Super Series
OPEN LEARNING FOR SUPERVISORY MAN

GW01085692

Technical Aspects of Supervision

No. 212

MANAGING TIME

Published
for
The National Examining Board for Supervisory Management
in conjunction with
The Northern Regional Management Centre

by
Pergamon Open Learning
a division of
Pergamon Press
Oxford · New York · Beijing · Frankfurt
São Paulo · Sydney · Tokyo · Toronto

U.K.	Pergamon Press plc, Headington Hill Hall, Oxford OX3 0BW, England
U.S.A.	Pergamon Press, Inc., Maxwell House, Fairview Park, Elmsford, New York 10523, U.S.A.
PEOPLE'S REPUBLIC OF CHINA	Pergamon Press, Room 4037, Quianmen Hotel, Beijing, People's Republic of China
FEDERAL REPUBLIC OF GERMANY	Pergamon Press GmbH, Hammerweg 6, D-6242 Kronberg, Federal Republic of Germany
BRAZIL	Pergamon Editora Ltda, Rua Eça de Queiros, 346, CEP 04011, Paraiso, São Paulo, Brazil
AUSTRALIA	Pergamon Press Australia Pty Ltd., P.O. Box 544, Potts Point, N.S.W. 2011, Australia
JAPAN	Pergamon Press, 5th Floor, Matsuoka Central Building, 1-7-1 Nishishinjuku, Shinjuku-Ku, Tokyo 160, Japan
CANADA	Pergamon Press Canada Ltd., Suite No. 271, 253 College Street, Toronto, Ontario, Canada M5T 1R5

First edition 1986

Reprinted 1987, 1989

British Library Cataloguing in Publication Data

Managing time.—(The Super series. Technical
aspects of supervision; no. 212)
1. Executives—Time management
I. National Examining Board for Supervisory Management
II. Northern Regional Management Centre   III. Series
658.4′093   HD38.2

ISBN 0-08-034055-5

This work was produced under an Open Tech contract with the Manpower Services Commission. The views expressed are those of the authors and do not necessarily reflect those of the MSC or any Government Department or the Publisher.

Project Manager: Pam Sear
Material Source: NRMC
Author: George Boak
Editor: Harry V. Pardue
Illustrations: Pergamon Press

CONTENTS

PART D   PERFORMANCE CHECKS

PART E   UNIT REVIEW

INTRODUCTION TO THE NEBSM SUPER SERIES

OPEN LEARNING

The Super Series has been designed as a text-and-tape presentation for those who prefer self-study or who cannot attend courses on a regular basis.

As an open learning student, you have the opportunity of making a selection of units from our list to match your own requirements and you can study them when and where you wish.

TUTORIAL SUPPORT

Each unit has been written in such a way that you can study on your own. Although the units are complete in themselves, in some cases they provide not only *knowledge* but the opportunity of developing *skills*. In order to gain these skills you will need to join with others working in small groups in a Support Centre approved by the National Examining Board for Supervisory Management (NEBSM).

These centres can also help with any queries that may arise from your study of the unit and offer facilities such as libraries, microcomputers and videos in addition to tutorial assistance both by telephone and in the Centre.

If you would like help in designing your own programme of study, take the FREE CONSULTATION voucher included with this unit to the OPEN LEARNING TUTOR at your nearest NEBSM Support Centre. The tutor will also be able to give you details of the fees payable for the use of the Centre's facilities and for tutorial assistance.

STUDY NOTES

INTRODUCTION

This Unit of Study, like all those in the 'Super Series' is specially designed for studying on your own. This means that you can work at your own pace, and where and when you like. If you have a query, need help or want to join a group in order to develop skills as well as knowledge, your nearest NEBSM Management Support Centre can help you.

STUDY METHODS

Where. You can listen to the tape in the car or at home. You can read the workbook anywhere. But if you want to get the most from it you need to be able to concentrate without distractions like conversation, TV or children! You will also need somewhere to keep your workbook, papers and tape recorder together and in order.

When. This is entirely up to you. The writers who prepared the Units think that you will be able to complete them in about eight hours, though don't be dismayed if it takes longer than this as we all learn different things at different speeds. The best way, of course, is to plan in advance and to set aside a certain time on certain days in order to complete the Unit satisfactorily.

If the Unit forms a part of a training course, or you are working for a NEBSM Management Module Award and want to join a group, you may need to take these into account when you decide on your timetable.

Perhaps the best advice is not to be too ambitious but start *regular* periods of study — say an hour at a time. This will yield far better results than occasional long periods.

How. Listen to the first side of the tape and then read the workbook, section by section.

This has Activities and Self-Checks and your success in these will indicate how well you are doing. If you find that you are not doing very well, go back over the text and try again. It may be that you were in too much of a hurry.

Make notes in the workbook, or in a file if you want to discuss them with a tutor, of key points, because actually writing them down is a very useful way of helping to memorise them. If you keep your tape recorder handy you can record ideas or queries as they occur to you.

References to books, videos and films are also made in this workbook for those who want to study in greater depth. The Support Centre or your local library will be able to supply copies.

CONCENTRATE ON WHAT YOU ARE STUDYING, READ AND LISTEN UNTIL YOU HAVE GRASPED THE MATTER NOT JUST FOR AN HOUR OR TWO BUT SO THAT IT REMAINS WITH YOU. And if you can discuss the facts and ideas with other people this will develop your understanding and help to retain them in your mind.

HELP!   Help is available from

- Yourself. Go back and try again. Don't give up. If you don't understand or sometimes find it hard going, go back to it at the beginning of your next study period.

- Your family or friends. Even if they don't understand the subject the act of discussing it sometimes clarifies the point in your mind.

- Your training staff at work.

- The Support Centre, by phone or a visit (but phone for an appointment on your first visit).

UNIT OBJECTIVES

As a supervisor you may have many demands upon your time. Some of these demands may come from your workteam, some from management, others from your fellow supervisors. To do a good job you need to use your time effectively, to respond to these demands and to act according to your priorities.

The purpose of this unit is to consider how you can make better use of your time. We will look at what can happen in certain cases if time is wasted, or if people are overloaded and do not have enough time. We will see how to avoid common difficulties, and how to get more control over how we use our time.

IN THIS UNIT WE WILL:

● identify the advantages of good time management;

● develop a method of deciding upon priorities;

● suggest ways in which you can plan and control your time;

● provide a means of identifying and dealing with barriers to being a good time manager.

AUDIO TAPE
Side 1

Before you continue through the unit, you should listen to Side 1 of the audio tape that accompanies the unit. You will find it useful if you refer to the unit objectives shown below whilst you listen to the tape. You may wish to make the objectives clearer to yourself by making a note or two on the page as you listen.

OBJECTIVES

When you have worked through this unit you will be BETTER ABLE TO:

● understand the benefits of better management of your time;

● clearly explain the priority of different demands on your time;

● set out the steps you can take to plan and control your time;

● analyse problems which may arise and explain how you might deal with them.

PART A
THE IMPORTANCE OF
MANAGING YOUR TIME

1. Introduction

As a supervisor, you will have many demands on your time, as a number of people and a range of tasks compete for your attention. How should you ration your time between these demands? What rules can you follow? How can you make the best use of your time and abilities? These are questions which this unit will help you to answer.

When you have completed this section you should be able to:

explain the aim of managing your time;

recognise problems that can be solved by time management;

understand the importance of managing your time.

2. Managing Your Time

Let us be clear about the terms we are using. 'Managing time' and 'time management' are both common terms. They mean the same thing, but what I understand by them and what you understand by them may be different. So let us establish what they mean.

ACTIVITY I   TIME GUIDE 5 MINUTES

Think about the term 'managing time' for a few minutes and then, in the space provided, write a description of what it means to you.

_____

_____

PART

1

Examples of how 'managing time' has been described are:

making the best use of time;

getting more done in the time available;

not wasting time on irrelevant things;

getting more control over time;

spending more time on the important parts of the job;

avoiding the last minute rush.

These are only examples, of course, and you may have described 'managing time' in a slightly different way. The examples look at things we might wish to DO:

making the best use of our time;

getting more done;

spending more time on the important things.

And things we might wish to AVOID:

not wasting time;

avoiding the last minute rush.

These are the two sides of better time management.

Now that we have considered what is involved in managing our time, let us try to sum up what is meant by the term.

MANAGING OUR TIME MEANS GETTING MORE CONTROL OVER HOW WE SPEND OUR TIME AND THEN MAKING SENSIBLE CHOICES ABOUT HOW WE USE IT.

Making sensible choices about how to use our time will mean avoiding some of the time wasters, and directing ourselves to productive, important activities.

3.   How to be a Better Time Manager

In order to manage our time we will need to think about:

EXTENSIONS
1 and 2
page 68

WHAT WE ARE TRYING TO ACHIEVE;

PART

WHAT STANDS IN THE WAY OF OUR ACHIEVING THIS.

Let us look at a common time management problem to see how this works in practice.

2

4. Crisis Management

John the firefighter . . .

John is not really a fireman nor anything like it!

He works in a factory, supervising a team which assembles electrical components. As a supervisor of long standing, John is also called upon by management when problems arise on other assembly lines.

As he himself says:

"I never seem to have a minute to spare from eight in the morning to half-past four. Management always want everything done yesterday. 'There's a problem here, John. Sort it out, will you?' Or, 'Can you just check on stocks there, John, it's vital!' Or, 'We need five hundred chokes by Wednesday, John, it's urgent, top priority! How soon can you get the machines set up for a new batch?' I tell you, everything in this place is always top priority."

This kind of rushing from one crisis to the next, coping with whatever problem is most pressing at the time, is often called fire-fighting.

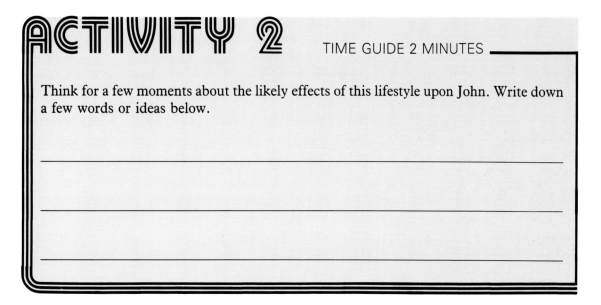

ACTIVITY 2   TIME GUIDE 2 MINUTES

Think for a few moments about the likely effects of this lifestyle upon John. Write down a few words or ideas below.

John is a true firefighter, dealing with one 'crisis' after another. The effects of this are likely to be:

STRESS. Because he is always dealing with 'top priority', 'vital', 'urgent' matters, John is likely to suffer from stress. Our ability to deal with stress varies from person to person, but where we

    always have to rush to get things done,

    know that if we fail to do the right thing we may be criticised,

then stress is likely to have unpleasant results.

It will cause fatigue, it may result in minor illnesses — as our resistance to colds or viruses is lowered — and over a longer period of time may result in major illnesses, affecting the heart or the stomach.

MISTAKES. Mistakes can come about when we try to do things in a hurry because

we don't check on things, on what we have been told (for example, the instructions we have been given), on what we see (for example, the stock levels);

we don't make the best decisions, because we don't take time to think things through.

We have described John as a 'firefighter'. Another description of him would be a 'crisis manager'. Of course, even in the best of companies, crises do occur. A true crisis is AN EVENT WITH IMPORTANT CONSEQUENCES WHICH UNEXPECTEDLY AND SUDDENLY ARISES.

Not all crises are TRUE crises. Some would not be UNEXPECTED if people looked a little way ahead. Some are not really as IMPORTANT as they are made out to be.

Some 'crises', in fact, are not really crises at all.

ACTIVITY 3   TIME GUIDE 5 MINUTES

Why do some people seem to create crises for themselves, or for other people to deal with? Write TWO suggestions in the space provided.

_____

_____

The attraction of 'firefighting' is so common that it has been identified as a regular method of working — 'management by crisis'. Reasons why management by crisis is so common seem to be:

it can be exciting;

dealing with crises can make people feel important;

it can make people feel that they have really achieved something (often that they have prevented a disaster);

it can be easier to get other people to do things if the situation is seen to be critical.

Check to see if your two suggestions are along the lines of the examples given here. If not, do you agree with my examples?

Despite the attractions of firefighting, it brings with it the twin problems of STRESS and MISTAKES, and we must beware of these dangers.

Let us remember what we need to think about in order to manage our time:

PART

WHAT WE ARE TRYING TO ACHIEVE;

WHAT STANDS IN THE WAY OF OUR ACHIEVING THIS.

ACTIVITY 4

TIME GUIDE 10 MINUTES

Think for a few moments about the FIRST STEPS John the firefighter should take in order to manage his time. Write a few words or ideas in the space provided.

_____

_____

_____

_____

_____

John should think about what he is trying to achieve. This will not be particularly easy. Like most of us, he is likely to have a number of goals. So he needs to consider his priorities in relation to these goals.

Because he is being told to do one thing after another, he may find it useful to talk to his manager about the priority of different jobs, to see if they are both in agreement.

He needs to consider if there are any goals he is not reaching. If this is so, then what could he do in order to reach them?

He could consider whether there is a particular problem which uses a great deal of his time. Is this time well spent, or is it a distraction?

These are some suggestions as to what John could do — you may well have thought of some more. I would suggest to John that the first steps in managing his time would involve using ALL of the suggestions above.

ACTIVITY 5

TIME GUIDE 3 MINUTES

Why does John need to take up all four suggestions to improve his time management?

_____

_____

_____

PART

5

The first two suggestions are about making sure that John knows what he should be trying to achieve.

The second two suggestions are about looking at what might be preventing him from reaching his goals.

Both sets of suggestions need to be followed if John is to start to manage his time better.

Before we leave crisis management, let us remind ourselves what 'crisis' really means.

SELF CHECK 1
TIME GUIDE 5 MINUTES

1. Do crises occur in the best of firms?   YES/NO

2. What is a true crisis?

    _____

    _____

3. Why are some 'crises' not really crises at all?

    _____

    _____

RESPONSE CHECKOUT

Crises do occur in the best of firms, because a time crisis is an event with important consequences which unexpectedly and suddenly arises. What are sometimes treated as crises aren't really. They can be created because people feel that management by crisis is exciting, adds to their feeling of importance and of having achieved something, and it may be easier to get others to do something if the situation seems to be critical.

5. Beck and Call

Managing our time means more than just avoiding crisis management. Let us look at another example.

Frances is a supervisor in a busy supermarket, in charge of a workteam of fourteen shop assistants. Frances is responsible to the store manager, Margaret, and she is supposed to liaise with the deputy store manager, Jim, on staffing details, stocks and customer information.

When the supermarket is busy, such as on a Saturday morning, all of Frances' workteam are on the check-out tills, or at the service counters. Frances spends most of her time in this part

PART

6

of the store telling check-out staff the prices of goods which have lost their price tags, fetching change, filling the tills and so on. At quieter times of the week there may be only two people on the tills, and Frances may supervise the re-stocking of shelves, or hold meetings with Margaret or Jim. On most days, she finds her shift passes quickly, and she walks many miles around the store, from one section to the next, dealing with minor problems, requests, queries, checking-in at the office and at the store-room out at the back. As she says: "Towards the end of the week, there's not much time to sit down and think about what I'm doing. I'm in charge of fourteen people — there are twenty-five staff in the store altogether — and then there are the reps and, of course, the customers. I'm just at everyone's beck and call."

She is quite cheerful about this. "I enjoy it best", she says, "when it's busy."

ACTIVITY 6   TIME GUIDE 15 MINUTES

1. Do you think Frances needs to manage her time better?   YES/NO

2. How could we find out the best way for Frances to manage her time?

_____

_____

Frances does not have an obvious problem, like John the firefighter had. From what we know of her so far, it is hard to say whether she could manage her time more effectively. We would need to consider:

> what her goals are;

> whether she is actually achieving them.

We need to think about an important principle here.

ACTIVITY 7   TIME GUIDE 1 MINUTE

Is time management only for people like John, who have obvious problems?

YES/NO

I suggest that time management is NOT just for people like John. Remember that we have suggested that managing time means

PART

MAKING THE BEST USE OF OUR TIME.

7

It follows, then, that managing time means

DEALING WITH THE PROBLEMS CAUSED BY
AN OVERLOAD OF WORK

and

TAKING ADVANTAGE OF OPPORTUNITIES WITHIN OUR REACH.

So, how could we discover the best way for Frances to manage her time?

WE NEED TO CONSIDER POSSIBLE PROBLEMS AND OPPORTUNITIES.

Supervisors who lead a 'beck and call' life at work frequently neglect longer-term goals. This is because they are so busy responding to the demands of the moment. By doing this, they can run into problems or they can miss opportunities.

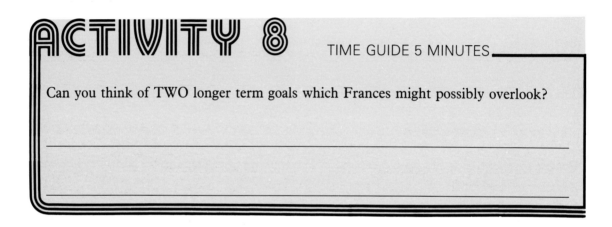

ACTIVITY 8   TIME GUIDE 5 MINUTES

Can you think of TWO longer term goals which Frances might possibly overlook?

_____

_____

Examples of goals Frances might neglect are:

    staff training;

    improving/maintaining staff morale;

    preparing for her own development, or possible promotion;

    getting involved in planning improved shelf layouts.

These are examples of activities leading to longer-term goals. There will be no immediate results from actions in these areas.

You may object to one of these examples. What if Frances has no interest in promotion? (Or, what if there are no opportunities?)

Yes, it is true that we would need to consider the goals of the particular person involved. In the same way, we need to give careful thought to our own goals, to the problems that may beset us, and to the opportunities that may be available.

PART

SELF CHECK 2

Respond by completing each sentence with a suitable word or words.

1. Managing time means dealing with the _____ caused by an _____ of work, and

2. taking _____ of _____ within our reach.

3. To discover the best way to manage our time we need to _____ _____ _____ _____ _____.

4. Supervisors who lead a 'beck and call' life at work frequently neglect _____ _____ goals.

RESPONSE CHECKOUT

Managing time means dealing with the problems caused by an overload of work, and taking advantage of opportunities within our reach. To discover the best way to manage our time, we need to consider possible problems and opportunities. Supervisors who lead a 'beck and call' life at work frequently neglect longer-term goals.

6. The Treadmill

Let us consider a final case.

Eve is an office supervisor in the planning department of a local authority. The workload varies in a regular fashion, going in five-week cycles. The final week in the cycle is very busy, but the pace of work is quite steady the rest of the time. The work which the office handles is quite simple and repetitive, and Eve sometimes envies people who (like John the firefighter) have an exciting time of it at work. Her own job, she says, "is like being on a treadmill. You jog along every day, but you never seem to get anywhere. Some mornings, it's an effort to get out of bed and come to work to switch on the machine." Things may change in the office in the future, as a computerised filing system is being brought in, but the planner in charge of the installation is overworked, and it is taking a long time.

PART

9

ACTIVITY 9

Do you think Eve could benefit from thinking about how to manage her time?

YES/NO

How could we find out the best way for Eve to manage her time?

_____

_____

Yes, it seems likely that Eve would benefit from thinking about how to manage her time.

As with Frances, we would need to consider:

> what are Eve's goals?

> is she actually achieving them?

> what are the problems and opportunities around Eve?

Supervisors who feel work is a treadmill frequently fail to see opportunities around them. Although work does not provide interesting challenges, they can feel under stress because of frustration.

When Eve considers her goals, and the problems and opportunities around her, she may feel that the best course of action is to start applying for another job! She may also be able to see some opportunities within reach around her, though, and may make use of them — for example she might get more involved in the new computerised filing system.

If we are 'on a treadmill' we may feel dissatisfied at the end of the day, because we seem to have achieved little or nothing. This is the main feature of the treadmill — although if you work as a 'firefighter' or you are at everyone's beck and call, you may feel this, too. We all want a certain amount of satisfaction from our working lives. If we don't get this, we feel that we are wasting our time.

ACTIVITY 10

TIME GUIDE 5 MINUTES

Suppose you went into work the other day with a list of ten things to do. Another matter cropped up, and at the end of the day, there are still six things on your list you have not done. You feel frustrated by this. What should you do? Write two suggestions in the space below.

_____

_____

PART

This looks like a 'no progress' situation. It is the sort of thing that puts people off trying to plan their time at all. What should you do? Here are some suggestions.

Remind yourself about what you *have* done. It may not have been what you intended to do, but you will have achieved something. Remind yourself of this.

Think about when you will be able to do the six remaining items. It is usually better to write them out again on a new list, as this makes you think about them in a positive way, as things you *do* intend to do.

Ask yourself this question: Was I being too optimistic in hoping to do all ten things today?

If the answer is 'yes', then maybe you need to draw up a shorter list for tomorrow! Or you could have a list of the same length, but remind yourself that if you do only *five* things, then you are doing quite well!

SELF CHECK 3   TIME GUIDE 10 MINUTES

1. What are the THREE questions we need to ask to find the best way of managing our time?

   _____

   _____

   _____

2. Fill in the missing words in these statements.

   a) Supervisors who feel work is a treadmill frequently fail to see _____.

   b) Although work does not provide interesting challenges they can feel _____ _____ because of _____.

PART

11

7.   The Activity Trap

We have looked at three cases where people could manage their time better, and the problems associated with each case.

Firefighting

Main problems: Stress.
                 Mistakes are made.

Beck and Call

Main problems: Longer-term goals are not reached.
                 Opportunities are overlooked.

The Treadmill

Main problems: Stress through frustration.
                 Opportunities are overlooked.

Each of these cases provides an example of the activity trap.

When we fall into the activity trap we

spend most of our time simply responding to the next, or the most pressing, demand upon our time WITHOUT thinking about what we are trying to achieve.

The danger of the activity trap, in other words, is that we lose sight of what we are trying to achieve. And the danger of doing *that* is that we run the risk of achieving nothing very much at the end of the day!

The way out of the activity trap, then, is to focus upon

GOALS.

PART

In other words, what we wish to achieve. And

PRIORITIES.

In other words, the relative importance of these goals.

Then we must make DECISIONS about how to use our time.

SELF CHECK 4   TIME GUIDE 10 MINUTES

Fill in the missing words in these statements.

1. The danger of the activity trap is that we lose sight of _____.

2. The way out of the activity trap is to focus upon

    a) _____ and

    b) _____.

3. Then we must make _____ about how to use our time.

RESPONSE CHECKOUT

1. 'What we are trying to achieve'. You may have written 'goals' or 'the end result'. Either of these would be correct.

2. a) The answer as for 1, will fit here!

    b) 'Priorities'. You may have written 'the relative importance of our goals', which would be correct.

3. 'Decisions'. It is important to realise that we do make decisions about how we use our time. This is the first step in really bringing it under our control. We will look at decisions in the next section.

8. Summary

● MANAGING TIME — means getting more control over how we spend our time and then making sensible choices about how we use it, so that we:

MAKE THE BEST USE OF OUR TIME;

DEAL WITH PROBLEMS CAUSED BY AN OVERLOAD OF WORK;

TAKE ADVANTAGE OF OPPORTUNITIES WITHIN OUR REACH.

PART

- TO MANAGE TIME EFFECTIVELY — we must think about:
  what we are trying to achieve;

  what stands in the way of our achieving this.

- A TRUE CRISIS — is an event with important consequences which unexpectedly and suddenly arises.

- But CRISIS MANAGEMENT — 'Firefighting' causes stress and mistakes.

- 'BECK AND CALL' — means that longer-term goals are neglected and opportunities are overlooked.

- 'THE TREADMILL' — causes stress through frustration and means opportunities are overlooked.

- THE ACTIVITY TRAP — means we respond without thinking ahead. The way out of the activity trap is to:

  focus on what we want to achieve;

  decide on priorities;

  make decisions about how to use our time.

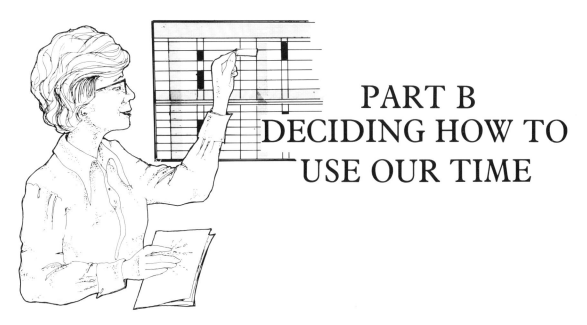

PART B
DECIDING HOW TO USE OUR TIME

1. Introduction

We have seen that time management means making decisions about how to spend our time, based on goals and priorities.

In this part of the unit, we will look at the process of making decisions. We will then concentrate on how you can analyse the demands upon your time.

2. Decision-making

Let us make sure that we are both talking about the same thing when we talk about decision-making. This is important because its meaning is central to this section.

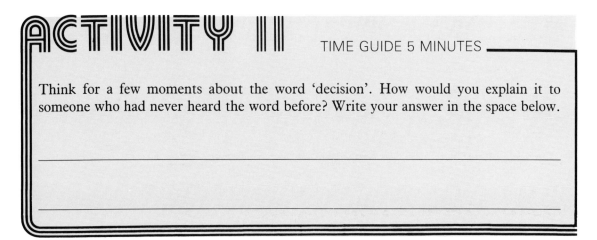

ACTIVITY 11   TIME GUIDE 5 MINUTES

Think for a few moments about the word 'decision'. How would you explain it to someone who had never heard the word before? Write your answer in the space below.

A decision can be defined as:

a choice between alternatives;

what happens when someone picks one option rather than another;

a selection of one thing rather than another;

a preference for one thing rather than another;

what happens when a person opts for one thing rather than another;

what happens when a person elects to do one thing rather than another.

The main thing about a decision is that there is more than one thing that can be chosen. We are faced with a number of alternatives or options.

Why is this important to time management?

The main reason this is important to time management is because we will have choices about how to spend our time, and we need to make sure we are choosing the right options.

As a supervisor, you will be familiar with decisions. You will make decisions every hour of every day — big decisions and small decisions. Most decisions go through a series of stages, although, with the smaller decisions we may go through these stages so quickly that we are hardly aware of them.

ACTIVITY 12   TIME GUIDE 10 MINUTES

Suppose you are supervisor in the production area of a manufacturing company. You've been instructed by your manager to keep overtime to an absolute minimum, but, on Thursday morning, you receive a rush order from sales which you know you can't meet this week without overtime. You could probably meet the order the following week, but sales want the goods by Monday. You could organise some overtime for Thursday and Friday and risk your boss being annoyed that his instructions were ignored, or you could leave a decision until Friday when he'll be back from a business trip and get him to authorise weekend working. Weekend working would cost the company more than overtime on Thursday and Friday. One way or another you have to make a decision.

Jot down *the stages* by which you would reach a decision. *What* you would decide isn't important — it's the stages which your thinking would go through before you carried out your decision that we're interested in.

_____

_____

_____

_____

_____

You have probably felt that you would need more information before you could make a decision.

Do sales really need the order in full by Monday?

Could you supply a part-order now, and schedule the rest for next week?

If so, what is the minimum they need now, and the maximum you can let them have?

Could you rearrange the work you have scheduled for this week?

There's a lot you would need to know and this is the first stage of the decision-making process.

This is called the *knowledge stage*.

The Knowledge Stage

Here you are asking:

What is the situation?

What is the problem to be solved?

What is the background to the problem?

For a small decision, you may already have all the knowledge you need — all you have to do is to think about it. For some decisions, you may have to find out information; by talking to people, or by doing some reading. Sometimes, this stage is known as the *finding-out* stage, or the *assessment* or *appraisal* stage. Because many decisions are brought about by problems which have arisen, this is also sometimes called the *problem definition* stage. When we think about long-term decisions it is sometimes called the *forecasting* stage.

Having found out enough information to form an accurate idea of what the problem involves, you can then decide exactly what you're trying to do.

In our case, perhaps it's deciding exactly how much extra you have to produce this week, and next.

We can call this stage the *objective stage*.

The Objective Stage

Here you are asking:

What am I trying to achieve?

This is an important stage. Check that you have mentioned it, or something like it (say, goals, aims, end results or purpose).

Then you would have to decide which courses of action are open to you: overtime now; shelving a decision until the manager comes back and then perhaps having to work weekend overtime; not scheduling the order in full until the following week.

This stage is the *alternatives stage*.

PART

17

The Alternatives Stage

Here you are asking:

What can I do?

What are the alternatives/options which are open to me?

After that you have to weigh up the advantages and disadvantages of each possible course of action.

We can call this the *look-ahead stage*.

The Look-ahead Stage

Here you are asking:

How would these alternatives work out?

How far would they go in meeting my objectives?

What would the cost of each alternative be?

You may have included this in your alternatives stage. Other words used to describe this stage are *estimating stage* or *previewing stage*. Basically, we are trying to predict the possible results of our decisions, in order to choose the best alternative.

Finally, you have to choose one of the possible courses of action — arranging overtime for Thursday and Friday, for instance — and get on with it.

This stage is called the *action stage*.

The Action Stage

Here you are choosing one of your alternatives, putting it into practice and seeing how it works out. If it is not successful then you may have to make another decision. This is sometimes called the *implementation stage*, or the *implementation and evaluation stage*.

We may not go through these stages step-by-step, one after another, in a mechanical fashion. When a problem arises we may think about objectives, alternatives and background information in a different order, as all sorts of things pass through our mind.

Each stage is essential to making a good decision, though. When we are under pressure we may fail to:

make sure we know all the relevant facts;

think about our goals (and fall into the *activity trap*);

see the alternatives available to us;

think these alternatives through.

PART

The way I have described the stages is:

KNOWLEDGE;

OBJECTIVES;

ALTERNATIVES;

LOOKING AHEAD;

ACTION.

If we take the first letter of each word, we make the acronym KOALA, which spells the name of an Australian bear (not, incidentally, known for its decisiveness!). This is an easy way to remember the five stages.

3.   Deciding How to Use Our Time

There are three ways in which our time gets used up:

We respond to the demands which other people place on us.

We do things out of habit.

We can make realistic decisions about how to use it.

**BECOMING BETTER AT MANAGING OUR TIME MEANS MAKING
REALISTIC DECISIONS ABOUT MORE AND MORE OF IT.**

We have thought about the stages in making decisions. Let us look at the other two 'governors' of our time — the demands of other people and our own habits.

4.   Responding to Demands

As a supervisor there may be many people who make demands on your time. You may try to ration your time evenly between these demands, or you may concentrate on some, and ignore others altogether.

Any attempt at making better use of your time must begin from your current position — the way you use your time at present.

ACTIVITY 13

Think about who makes demands on your time at the present, and what they expect you to do. Write this down in the space provided below. I have written an example, which will probably apply to you, to get you started.

WHO	WHAT
Workteam	To deal with any problems arising from breakdown of machinery.

PART

Some further examples of demands upon your time may be:

WHO	WHAT
Workteam	To give clear instructions about tasks.
	To give training in new tasks.
	To talk with them about any proposed changes.
	To take an interest in them.
	To help them with problems.
Management	To supervise the workteam effectively (including training and discipline).
	To ensure good production.
	To provide information about production.
	To provide advice about the effects of any proposed changes.
	To be knowledgeable about any legislation, industrial relations agreements or working practices that may affect your workteam.
	To liaise with others, as necessary.
Inspection/Quality control	To supervise the workteam so as to produce goods up to acceptable standards.
	To talk with inspectors about any problems discovered.
Trade union representatives	To discuss any grievances or disciplinary matters.
	To discuss any planned changes.

Some of these examples may not apply to your own case. Check your list, however, and make sure you have listed all the different PEOPLE who make demands upon your time.

So far, we have only thought about the demands which are made on you at work. But social and family life can suffer if we give too much time to our work. For example, our family life can suffer if we use quite a lot of time, particularly in the evenings, thinking about work problems — or simply resting after a long, hard day!

What we have done is to look at the general picture. But, in any particular week, or on any particular day, or any particular hour, the people around you may be making specific demands.

As a practising supervisor, you will know that sometimes you cannot respond to all of these demands. For example, suppose you have started some on-the-job training with a member of your team and a member of management turns up, wanting to talk to you. You are not able to do both things at once. One of the demands cannot be met at that point in time.

PART

Sometimes, the problem is easy to resolve. Suppose two members of your workteam want to talk to you, at the same time, about problems they have. They both want a private word with you. You can simply ask one to wait while you talk to the other.

Often the problems are not so simple. Suppose you are trying to plan the work schedule for the following week, but you are constantly interrupted by visits from your workteam and calls from management. If you are going to do a good job, the planning activity requires you to give it some careful thought. It may be much more important than any of the visits or calls, but they are much more immediate and you have to respond to them, so the planning doesn't get done, or it gets postponed, or gets done badly.

Do you remember the types of time management problems we looked at in Part A?

Crisis management

Beck and call

The treadmill

Here to remind you is how people working in those ways described their typical working day.

Crisis Management

"I never seem to have a minute to spare from eight in the morning to half-past four. Management always want everything done yesterday. 'There's a problem here, John. Sort it out will you?' Or, 'Can you just check on stocks there, John, it's vital.' Or, 'We need five hundred chokes by Wednesday, John, it's urgent, top priority! How soon can you get the machines set up for a new batch?' I tell you, everything in this place is always top priority."

Beck and Call

When the supermarket is busy, such as on a Saturday morning, all of Frances' workteam are on the check-out tills, or at the service counters. Frances spends most of her time in this part of the store telling check-out staff the prices of goods which have lost their price tag, fetching change, filling the tills and so on. At quieter times of the week there may be only two people on the tills, and Frances may supervise the re-stocking of shelves, or hold meetings with Margaret or Jim. On most days, she finds her shift passes quickly, and she walks many miles around the store, from one section to the next, dealing with minor problems, requests, queries, checking in at the office and the store-room out at the back. As she says: "Towards the end of the week there's not much time to sit down and think about what I'm doing. I'm in charge of fourteen people — there are twenty-five staff in the store altogether — and then there are the reps and of course, the customers. I'm just at everyone's beck and call."

She is quite cheerful about this. "I enjoy it best", she says, "when it's busy."

The Treadmill

Eve is an office supervisor, in the planning department of a local authority. The workload varies in a regular fashion, going in five-week cycles. The final week in the cycle is very busy, but the pace of work is quite steady the rest of the time. The work which the office handles is quite simple and repetititve, and Eve sometimes envies people who (like John the firefighter) have an exciting time of it at work. Her own job, she says, "is like being on a treadmill. You jog along every day, but you never seem to get anywhere. Some mornings, it's an effort to get out of bed and come to work to switch on the machine." Things may change in the office in the future, as a computerised filing system is being brought in, but the planner in charge of the installation is overworked, and it is taking a long time.

ACTIVITY 14

TIME GUIDE 20 MINUTES

What kind of demands are placed upon the supervisors in each of those cases? I have described the demands on the crisis manager to give you a start, so think about beck and call, and the treadmill.

The crisis manager

A large number of demands.

Most, or all, of the demands are said to be urgent and important.

Most, or all, of the demands seem to come from management.

The need for longer-term planning activities seems to be ignored.

Beck and call

_____

_____

_____

_____

The treadmill

_____

_____

_____

_____

The kinds of demands placed on the supervisors in the other two cases can be described like this:

Beck and call

A large number of demands.

Many of the demands are about small matters.

PART

The demands come from management, the workteam and other people.

Longer-term goals may be neglected.

The treadmill

A large volume of demands.

The demands are mostly of the same type — there is a high workload, without the variety of the crisis manager or beck and call.

The demands seem to be regular and predictable.

Longer-term goals may be neglected.

You may have made other points about the demands made upon these people. But I hope you'll agree that mine are also true.

This activity stresses the fact that one of the main things to suffer when we have many demands on our time is the achievement of longer term goals. It is all too easy to become like a sailing ship without a pilot, blown first this way and then the other.

What can we do about this?

WE MUST MAKE REALISTIC DECISIONS ABOUT HOW WE RESPOND TO DEMANDS.

The first step in doing this is to think about our OBJECTIVES. Which of the demands on our time are important to achieving these objectives?

One of the discoveries we may make when we ask this question is that we should be spending some time on tasks which no one is actually requiring us to do.

Think about what you are doing right now. You are working through a unit that is part of a programme which will improve the way you do your job. Has anyone required you to do this? Probably not. It is a demand which you have made of yourself.

Most of us, then, know that:

WE SHOULD DO MORE THAN JUST RESPOND TO THE DEMANDS OF OTHER PEOPLE.

In Part C we will see that there are some practical methods you can use to deal with the demands of other people. For the time being, let us turn our attention to habit, and to making realistic decisions about how we use our time.

Before we do that, you might like to think over this section, with the help of this next self check.

PART

SELF CHECK 5

a) What are the three ways in which our time gets used up?

_____

_____

_____

Fill in the gaps in the following statements.

b) One of the main things to suffer when we have many demands on our time is the

achievement of _____ _____ _____ .

c) What we can do about this is to make _____ _____
about how we respond to demands.

d) Most of us know that we should do more than just _____ to the

_____ of other people.

RESPONSE CHECKOUT

a) Time gets used up responding to the demands of other people, out of habit and in making realistic decisions.

b) It is the achievement of *longer-term goals* which suffer when we have many demands on our time.

c) So we have to make realistic decisions about how we respond to demands.

d) Most of us know that we should do more than just respond to the demands of other people.

5. Habits

Habits are routines. Habits are repeated patterns of behaviour. When we do something automatically, we are probably doing it out of habit.

Some people are 'creatures of habit' — they are comfortable with the same routines, each day or each week. From time to time any of us may feel that we are 'in a rut' — meaning that we are unhappy with what is around us and the way we habitually respond to it.

PART

Habits are a necessary part of our lives, they help to keep us organised, they help to keep us satisfied. When we break them we can feel uncomfortable, or uneasy.

Let us consider how habits can operate at work.

Bill is a supervisor in charge of a 'general duties' team in a factory. Part of the work of the team is to keep the factory floor clean. There are also a variety of other jobs which they may be asked to tackle. Bill organises the work so that the team know they are supposed to sweep the floors in the morning. They then report to Bill after lunch for any special jobs which need to be done.

In the morning, Bill checks once or twice on the work of his team. He can talk to some of the operators on the production lines, spend a few minutes with each of his fellow supervisors, and talk to his manager. There is time to do any planning activities in the latter half of the morning, when he is not busy directly supervising the work of his team.

Bill can organise his time so that his team know what they are supposed to be doing in the mornings, and they make very few demands on his time. He sees other people at regular times in the morning and keeps himself informed, and he has time to work on longer term activities. Establishing a routine has helped him to make good use of his time. He is an example of the rule that:

GOOD HABITS CAN HELP TO MAKE THE BEST USE OF OUR TIME.

They can also help other people to relate to us. Bill's manager knows that Bill will drop by his office at a certain time each morning; the other supervisors know that they will see Bill at a certain time each day; so do his workteam. If anyone has anything to take up with Bill, it will usually wait until they see him. Everyone knows that between eleven and twelve is a bad time to try to see Bill, as he is normally busy. He comes up with good ideas for training, for jobs his team could tackle, and suggestions about how things could be improved. He calls the hour before lunch his 'thinking time', and firmly but (usually) politely discourages people from interrupting him then.

From the sound of Bill's job, he might fall into the *treadmill* category of problem. Yet he is thoughtful (and possibly fortunate) enough to be able to make a certain time of day his own, when he can concentrate on longer term goals.

ACTIVITY 15   TIME GUIDE 10 MINUTES

Bearing in mind the example you have just read, think for a few moments about how habits can help us to make the best use of our time at work and jot down three possible ways.

_____

_____

_____

PART

26

Habits can help us when:

they establish routines that enable us to get our work done;

they help us to achieve our goals, both long-term and short-term;

they help us to fit in with the people who make demands on our time.

These are three GENERAL points about helpful habits. You may have suggested some examples — check to see whether your examples fit into one or more of the general categories I have mentioned.

You may notice that, in Bill's case, when we talk about his habits helping him to fit in with people who make demands on his time, there is a bit of give and take. Bill fits in with other people's schedules (like his manager and the other supervisors), and tries to make sure that they will fit in with his.

Let us now consider an example of habits that are *not* helpful at work.

John, the crisis manager from Part A, was a supervisor who would take on anything that came his way. He had worked for a long time with a manager who was careful not to overload him. Then that manager left, to be replaced by a younger man who tended to panic even in a minor crisis.

John's habit was a simple one. He would listen to his manager's instructions and say no more than "I'll see to it", then off he would dash to deal with the problem.

When other supervisors were given the same instructions they might raise difficulties, or point out that they had their hands full at the moment. So the manager turned more and more often to John, with more and more jobs for him to do. And John carried on behaving like a willing horse — saying no more than "I'll see to it".

In a way this small habit meant that John created many of his own problems.

ACTIVITY 16 TIME GUIDE 3 MINUTES

Think for a few moments about how habits can lead us to make poor use of our time. Jot down two suggestions in the space below.

_____

_____

PART

27

Habits can get in the way when:

they lead us to do things which are not important to our job, or to waste time;

they do not help us to achieve our goals;

they do not help us to fit in properly with the people who make demands on our time.

You can see that these are three general points. If you have given examples, then check to see whether they fit into one or more of these general categories.

You may think that in John's case he is achieving one of his goals — that of keeping his manager happy. But John is likely to have other goals. Should he abandon all his other goals for the sake of this one?

I would suggest: not if he can help it. You can see that John's case is an example of someone who does not fit in properly with the people who make demands on his time, because he gives up control of his time in order to jump to their command. Some supervisors may go to the other extreme. Their routines are so rigid that they *always* appear unhelpful and so they don't fit in, either.

We have seen that habits can be helpful or unhelpful in managing our time. It can be useful to think about the things you do out of habit and ask yourself these questions:

How is this helping me to get my work done?

What goal is this helping me to reach?

How does this fit in with the people who make demands on my time?

The big danger with doing something out of habit is that we become blind to the alternatives — to the other things we could be doing instead. There may be better ways to use our time, but we do not consider them.

And unless we examine our habits, it is very difficult to change them so that we use our time more productively.

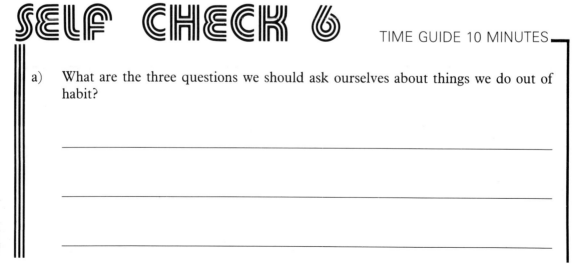

SELF CHECK 6 TIME GUIDE 10 MINUTES

a) What are the three questions we should ask ourselves about things we do out of habit?

_____

_____

_____

PART

B

b) Are habits always a bad thing if we want to manage our time better?

_____

c) What is the big danger with doing something out of habit?

_____

_____

RESPONSE CHECKOUT

a) When we do things out of habit we should ask ourselves: how is this helping me to get my work done? What goal is this helping me to reach? How does this fit in with the people who make demands on my time?

b) No. Sometimes they are very helpful. Good habits can help us to make the best use of our time.

c) We become blind to the alternatives. In other words, we stop making decisions about how to use our time.

6. Priorities

We have agreed that in order to make best use of our time we need to think in terms of

OBJECTIVES
and
PRIORITIES.

In this section let us think about priorities. What makes something a priority? What are the different types of priority?

ACTIVITY 17

TIME GUIDE 2 MINUTES

What do we mean when we say something is 'top priority'? Write your answer in the space below.

_____

_____

PART

B

When we say something is top priority we might mean:

it is very urgent and must be dealt with immediately;

it is very urgent and important, and it must be done immediately and done well;

it is very important and we should give a great deal of attention, or thought, to it;

it takes precedence over anything else.

Check that your answer is along the lines of one of the answers above.

In fact, when we look closely at the word, 'priority' it becomes less useful than we might have thought. You will probably find it more useful to think in terms of the things which make something a priority:

IMPORTANCE
and
URGENCY.

ACTIVITY 18   TIME GUIDE 4 MINUTES

Think for a few moments about what we mean when we say something is

urgent

important

What do we mean by each of them?

Write your answer in the space provided.

Urgent _____

_____

Important _____

_____

The fact of the matter is, the two words are often confused with one another, when really they represent quite different things.

Urgent — something is urgent when it has to be done by a certain time or we have a fixed deadline. The job becomes urgent as we approach the deadline.

PART

We can talk about things being more urgent or less urgent than others when they have different deadlines.

Suppose two of our tasks are:

to arrange holiday schedules for the next quarter for our workteam, the schedule to be submitted next Thursday;

to prepare a brief appraisal on a new member of the team, to be submitted next Tuesday.

Whatever the importance of the two tasks, the appraisal report is more urgent, because the deadline is closer. We could show this on a scale like this:

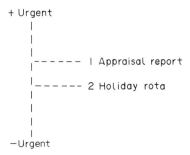

As the days pass, both jobs will become more urgent as they approach the deadline.

Important — something is important when it will have a big effect or a long-term effect upon our job, upon our career or concerns something which we value highly.

For example, we may know that it is necessary to prepare the holiday rota carefully, because it is difficult to change it and because the workteam take it very seriously. Whereas the appraisal report on the new member of staff may be only a formality. We have to write the report, but it is not going to say much or have much effect. So preparing the holiday rota is more important than writing the appraisal report.

(This, of course, is only an example. Your own organisation may take appraisal reports very seriously.)

SELF CHECK 7   TIME GUIDE 5 MINUTES

The difference between *importance* and *urgency* is central to good time management. So let's check what we mean by them once more.

What makes something *urgent*?

What makes something *important*?

_____

_____

_____

PART

Now let us combine the two ideas, urgency and importance, in the *time management grid*.

7.   The Time Management Grid

If we combine these two scales, urgency and importance, we have a grid, like this:

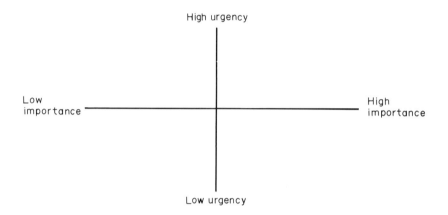

We can then be more precise about what we mean by a 'priority'. We could show our two
tasks as I have done on the grid below. We'll call the appraisal report Job 1 and the holiday
rota Job 2.

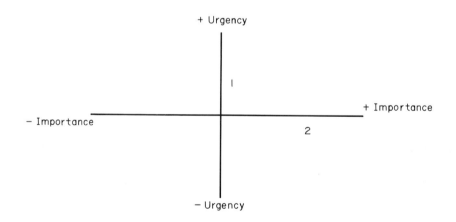

We can show the relative importance and urgency of the two tasks in this way.

ACTIVITY 19

Think about the way the tasks are presented on the grid. What do we gain from thinking about these tasks in this way? Jot down some ideas in the space below.

_____

_____

_____

_____

_____

The main thing we gain from thinking about these two tasks in this way is that we

DO NOT CONFUSE URGENCY WITH IMPORTANCE.

What else do we gain?

We are reminded that the appraisal report is more urgent than the holiday rota. So we may decide to do it before we do the holiday rota.

We are reminded that the holiday rota is more important, so we should spend more time on it, think more carefully about it, and make sure it is correct.

We can see that if, for some reason, we could only do ONE of these two things, we should do the holiday rota.

The time management grid is a very useful way of looking at demands upon your time. Whether they are demands which other people are making on you, or demands you are making on yourself, you can estimate their importance and their urgency.

It is not easy to separate urgency and importance, until you have had a little practice. Let us look at another problem.

PART

ACTIVITY 20

A job has been lying on your desk for a week. When it first came in, you decided it was at the first point on the grid below. You had more important things to do, and it has moved up, as the days pass, along the dotted line. Now it has to be done before lunchtime. Is it now *more important* to do it?

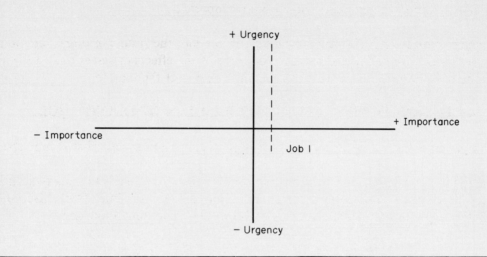

The answer is that it is probably not more important now. *THE PASSAGE OF TIME USUALLY ONLY MAKES THINGS MORE URGENT, NOT MORE IMPORTANT.*

ACTIVITY 21

What makes things more important?

Here is the time management grid again with one job entered.

All sorts of things could happen to make the job become more important and move to the right of the grid.

Using your own experience, jot down *one* reason which could make a job become more important.

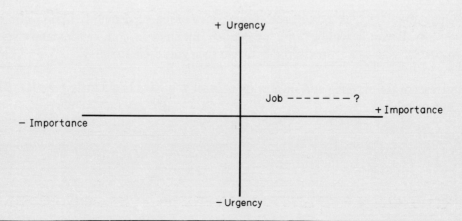

PART

Well, any number of things can make a job become more important.

Perhaps a new and potentially important customer wants a product or service which you can offer.

Perhaps if a certain project is successful, your team may be eligible for a special award.

Perhaps the managing director is taking a personal interest in a particular job.

Any of these would probably make the job more important.

If the managing director is showing an interest in the job, the results of doing the job may change. And, since we defined importance in terms of the effects of something, we can say that if something becomes important it is because we expect there to be

A CHANGE IN THE EFFECTS OR RESULTS OF DOING A JOB.

This example gives rise to a particularly thorny problem: who decides what is important?

If you are going to make sensible decisions about how to use your time, you must fix it in your mind that YOU decide the importance of the demands on your time. Otherwise you let opportunities slip. But you must remember *what* makes something important:

THE EFFECTS OF DOING THAT TASK.

If you ignore the interest of the managing director, for example, what may be the effects?

Loss of promotion chances?

A 'black mark' against you?

An official reprimand?

These things have to be taken into account if they will affect you in your particular job. They are likely to affect your decision.

ACTIVITY 22   TIME GUIDE 10 MINUTES

You have planned to spend some time today training two new members of your team. Your boss asks you to take on another job, which you think is less important. List THREE ALTERNATIVE things you could do.

_____

_____

_____

PART

I have asked you to think about ALTERNATIVES here to show that there is a decision to be made. Not all of the alternatives may be sensible to follow in your own case.

Here are some examples.

Tell your boss that you haven't time — that the training is urgent and important.

Tell your boss your plans for training, and point out the effect of not doing it. Argue that you consider the training more important.

Tell your boss your plans for training, and point out the effect of not doing it, but leave the decision with your boss.

Tell your boss your plans for training, but, if your boss tells you not to do the training today, you get him to agree a time when you will be able to do it.

Agree to do your boss's job, but make a strong case for having to take time to do the training before the end of the week.

Agree to do your boss's job without discussion.

Working in an organisation means that you are working under the direction of someone else. Sometimes the alternatives we could choose are limited by this. Often we cannot make decisions about how to use our time without the agreement of others. Some of the alternatives we have just looked at put us in the position of sharing the decision with our boss. We try to persuade the boss that we are right about what is important, by pointing out why we think something is important:

THE EFFECTS OF DOING OR (in this case) NOT DOING A JOB.

Now that we can think about demands upon our time in terms of their importance and urgency, let us look at four types of demands by looking at the four parts, or QUADRANTS, of the grid.

8.   The Quadrants

The time management grid is made up of four squares, or quadrants. There are certain common problems, or dangers, connected to demands upon our time which fall into each of these quadrants.

Let us look at each of these quadrants in turn, and identify the dangers. After all, forewarned is forearmed!

a)   Take the top right-hand quadrant:

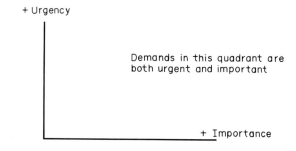

Tasks of this type get done, on the whole. The danger is:

THEY MAY NOT GET DONE VERY WELL.

This is because they may be done in a hurry, because they are close to a deadline. So they do not get the time and care they deserve. The top right-hand quadrant is the CRISIS SQUARE.

b) Take the bottom right-hand quadrant:

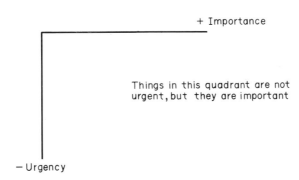

+ Importance

Things in this quadrant are not urgent, but they are important

– Urgency

There are two types of job in this quadrant:

jobs which have a deadline, but it is a long way in the future;

jobs which do not have a deadline at all.

The danger with jobs in this square is:

THEY MAY NOT GET DONE.

This is because there seems to be no urgency about them, although they are important.

If there is a deadline, but it is a long time in the future, then these jobs will gradually rise until they come into the *crisis square*, and you will have to do something about them.

If there is no deadline, then these are likely to be things which you see as being important, but nobody else does — yet! The danger is that you may NEVER get around to those things in that case.

People who suffer from the frustrations of the treadmill usually have a number of things at the bottom of this quadrant, which they never get around to doing. Good time managers spend a lot of time on jobs in this square. Because it contains jobs which may have a long-term effect we can call it the PLANNING SQUARE.

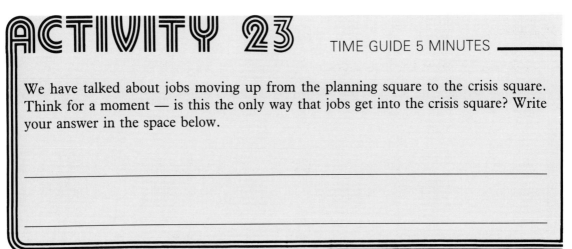

ACTIVITY 23 TIME GUIDE 5 MINUTES

We have talked about jobs moving up from the planning square to the crisis square. Think for a moment — is this the only way that jobs get into the crisis square? Write your answer in the space below.

_____

_____

PART

I suggest that some things can simply arrive in the crisis square, and there is no way to guard against them. Other things do rise from the planning square. The form of each supervisor's job is different of course, and you should think about how things come to be in your crisis square. Could they have been guarded against? What measures could you take to prevent similar crises occurring in the future?

c)   The top left-hand quadrant

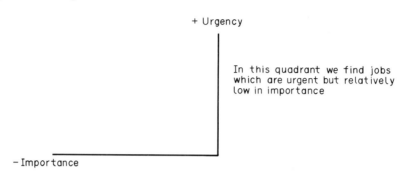

In this quadrant we find jobs which are urgent but relatively low in importance

These things tend to get done — because they are urgent. The danger is:

WE SPEND TOO MUCH TIME ON THEM.

This is time which we should spend on the more important parts of our job. Demands in this square should be dealt with quickly. To remind ourselves of this, let us call it the QUICK and SIMPLE SQUARE.

d)   The bottom left-hand quadrant

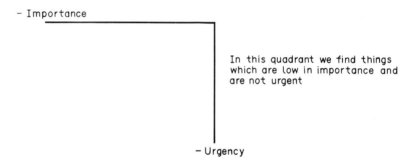

In this quadrant we find things which are low in importance and are not urgent

The danger here is:

WE SPEND TIME DOING THESE THINGS.

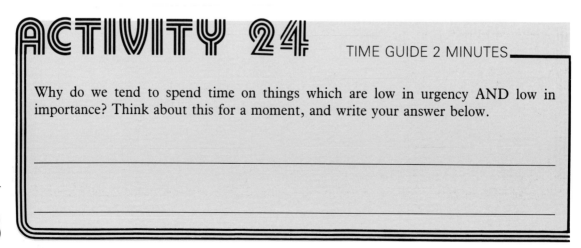

ACTIVITY 24   TIME GUIDE 2 MINUTES

Why do we tend to spend time on things which are low in urgency AND low in importance? Think about this for a moment, and write your answer below.

_____

_____

PART

B

Generally, these things get done because they are easy. We may spend time on them simply because they ARE easy, or they may be things we enjoy doing although they are not particularly important to the job.

As a general rule, it is usually better to leave these things until they become more urgent, especially if there are more important things to do. Certainly, we should be careful not to spend too much of our time doing things in that bottom left-hand square. To remind us to avoid this in future, let us call it the WASTE SQUARE.

We have looked at a way of analysing demands upon our time in terms of their importance and urgency.

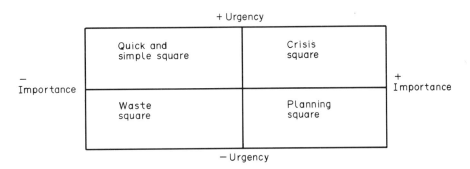

Before we move on from this, try the self check below.

SELF CHECK 8   TIME GUIDE 10 MINUTES

Think about the dangers associated with each of the squares in the time management grid. See if you can briefly write out each danger in the space provided.

Quick and simple square _____

_____

Crisis square _____

_____

Planning square _____

_____

Waste square _____

_____

PART

RESPONSE CHECKOUT

The *quick and simple square* means things are urgent but not important. The danger is that we may spend too much time on them.

The *crisis square* means things are urgent and important and the danger is that, although they may be done, they may not be done well.

The *planning square* means things are important but not urgent so there is a risk that they may be put off and not done until they reach crisis proportions.

The *waste square* means things are not important nor urgent but they may well be easy and it's a temptation to do them when we could more usefully be spending time on something else.

9. Summary

●   Decision-making is the key to managing time.

● Our time is governed by: OTHER PEOPLE'S DEMANDS;

                                    HABITS.

● Some habits, such as an orderly routine, help us to manage our time, but some may get in our way. All habits need to be reviewed critically.

● To make sound decisions we must think about:

            OBJECTIVES — what we are trying to achieve;

            PROPERTIES — distinguishing between what is important and what is urgent.

● We can look at the relative importance and urgency of various jobs by using a TIME MANAGEMENT GRID.

PART C
PLANNING AND
CONTROLLING
YOUR TIME

1. Introduction

We have seen that we should make decisions about how to use our time on the basis of the *importance* and *urgency* of demands upon us.

To put this into practice and become better managers of our time we need to think about:

how to plan our time;

how to adjust our plans to cope with unexpected problems.

In this part of the unit we will look at planning and controlling our time, and some of the things we will need to do to get our time under our own control.

When you have finished this part of the unit you should be able to:

make a daily plan;

put items on the plan in a sensible order;

allocate time to items on the plan;

explain how you could deal with REGULAR and RARE disruptions;

describe, and use, a time log;

describe the range of things you might need to do in order to manage your time.

PART

2. Planning Your Time

To make the best use of your time you are going to have to do some forward thinking or planning. Two of the basic tools of the good time manager are:

a diary;

a list system.

You are likely to require one or both of these. They are particularly helpful if you are in a job where there are a number of different demands upon your time. Signs of a bad time manager are a trail of missed appointments, broken promises and things which simply have not been done. A diary and a list system help you, and your memory, to avoid this.

The diary is for long-range planning — to note appointments and commitments for some time in the future. It will depend on your particular job whether you will have much need of this.

The list system can help you plan on a week-by-week, day-by-day basis. It is generally best to get into the habit of making a daily list at a particular time each day. First thing in the morning, or last thing at the end of the shift (in planning for the following day) are usually good times.

Let us suppose that at the start of the morning you make a list of the things you would like to do that day. You have made a start, in fact, on the knowledge and alternatives stages of the decision: how am I going to use my time today?

Once you have done this you will need to decide two things:

in what order you will tackle the items on your list;

how long you will spend on each item.

The next two sections deal with these decisions. Before you turn to them, though, let us think about the need for list systems.

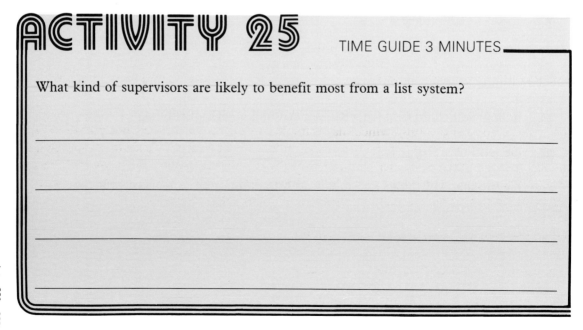

ACTIVITY 25   TIME GUIDE 3 MINUTES

What kind of supervisors are likely to benefit most from a list system?

_____

_____

_____

_____

There are a number of things which will affect how much you may benefit from a list system.

Supervisors in charge of a general duties team, who may tackle a number of different tasks, are particularly likely to benefit. If the workteam tackles routine tasks, day after day, then there is less planning required.

Supervisors who have to relate to a large number of people as part of their job are likely to benefit. The list can be used as a way of reminding them of matters which have to be taken up with each person.

Supervisors who are involved in any long-range projects can benefit from using a list system to plan the next steps they need to take.

Supervisors who have poor memories can benefit from using a list system too!

Check to see whether your suggestions are the same, or similar, to the types of supervisor I have mentioned. I hope we can agree that all the supervisors I have described would benefit from a list system.

3. Order Planning

You need to think about the order in which you will tackle the items on your list.

Some items on the list will have a fixed deadline, for example, a production report or a stock report which is due by a certain time of the day.

Some items on the list may have a natural deadline. Say, for example, you want one of your workteam to do a different job from the usual one today. You may wish to see them first thing in the morning.

When you have taken out the items which have

a fixed time,

a fixed deadline,

a natural deadline,

you may still be left with some items on the list. How do you decide when you are going to do these tasks?

There are a number of things which may influence this decision. Perhaps one part of the day is generally quiet, and you are likely to be undisturbed. This, then, would be a suitable time to plan on doing any item which requires thought and concentration. There may be times of the day when members of your workteam are likely to want your attention. Although this may not be an item on your list, you will need to take this into account.

There are two great dangers in order planning:

we do things in a certain order out of habit;

we do the easy, small or pleasant things first. The things in the waste square, in other words.

PART

This can be dangerous, because the important jobs may be:

difficult;

large;

unpleasant.

But they still need to be done, otherwise they wouldn't be important!

So, we need to be aware of these dangers in order planning, and be prepared to *make decisions about when to do things on the basis of their urgency and importance.* This is the general rule of order planning. It is a good idea to do the urgent things first, making sure that we have time somewhere to do things which may be important, but not particularly urgent.

Let us check back on order planning.

 **SELF CHECK 9** TIME GUIDE 15 MINUTES

a) Once you have made a list of things to do, what are the TWO things you will need to decide?

_____

_____

b) For each of the events below, say whether it is:

a fixed time;

a fixed deadline;

a natural deadline.

The health and safety representative has arranged an appointment with you for 2.30 pm.

_____

You have to get in touch with the wages department. You will need to do this before 1.00 pm, when returns are made up for the week.

_____

You need to get facts and figures about a proposed new machine before you see the health and safety representative.

_____

You want to talk to your chargehand about the progress your workteam is making, so you can decide what job to put them on in the afternoon.

_____

c) What is the general rule for order planning?

_____

_____

d) There are two great dangers in order planning. What are they?

_____

_____

_____

_____

4. Allocating Time

With our list of things to do in front of us, we now try to estimate how long each job will take. We may be proved wrong in the event, but in order to plan we have to make some kind of guess.

ACTIVITY 26

TIME GUIDE 5 MINUTES

Consider this question. When we have made our list of things to do, which do we do first — plan the order, or plan the time we will spend on each thing?

_____

_____

There is no hard and fast answer to this question. We should think about BOTH the *order* and the *amount of time* each item is likely to take. I suggest that you think first about the order, because in this way you think about the importance of each task, and your objectives. But you need to take into account the amount of time each task will take before making a final decision on what you are going to do.

When you have finished your planning, you will have a list of things you want to do, and the amount of time each is likely to take. You may find that, according to your estimates, you are going to have to do fourteen hours' worth of work in an eight-hour shift! If that is the case, at least you know it is unlikely that you will get everything done by the end of the day, unless you get some help.

Let us look at a typical problem.

ACTIVITY 27

TIME GUIDE 15 MINUTES

Suppose you are working on something which you have estimated will take two hours to complete. As you reach the end of that time, you realise that it is going to take you two *more* hours to finish. What do you do in this situation? Write some suggestions in the space below.

_____

_____

_____

_____

What you must do is to consider what is more important — finishing this task, or leaving it for the time being, and taking care of some of the other things you had planned to do.

It can be frustrating to have to leave something unfinished. If you are going to leave the job half-done, consider for a moment the amount of progress you have made. Just because you have not finished the job, as you planned, does not mean you have wasted your time. You will have made some progress.

Remember to think about what will not get done if you stick with this job until it is finished. Is there anything more urgent or important? Is there anything you could get someone else to do?

5. The Best-laid Plans . . .

Now that we have planned our day, we set about getting through the items on our list. On some days we may be very successful. Everything runs smoothly, and every item on the list is ticked off by the end of our shift. Other days we may come very close to completing every item. And then there are the days, when we have one of *those* days, and our planned day does not work out at all.

ACTIVITY 28   TIME GUIDE 5 MINUTES

Think for a moment about what kind of things can wreck your plans for the day. Jot down a few examples in the space below.

_____

_____

_____

Your examples are likely to be about something unexpected taking place. Here are the five *most common* examples of this:

there is an accident and one of your team, or a member of the public, needs your attention;

machinery breakdown stops your team working and means you are needed when you least expected it;

one of your team is absent and you lose time because of this;

an event which you had planned takes much longer than you expected;

someone, most likely your boss, gives you something extra to do.

See if your examples are the same, or similar to these. Don't worry if they are not. Your examples may point to particular problems you will have in planning your time. Identifying them as problems is the first step towards doing something about them.

PART

C

The five examples I have picked out are not all of the same type. We will look at each of them, briefly, in turn.

Before we do, let us consider the general rules about planning overtime and coping with the unexpected.

PLANS CANNOT ALWAYS BE ACHIEVED.

This doesn't mean that plans are worthless when we are faced with the unexpected.

PLANS CAN HELP US MAKE BETTER DECISIONS WHEN FACED WITH THE UNEXPECTED.

Because in making the plans we have thought about the urgency and importance of the tasks ahead of us. We can adjust our plans in a sensible way, then, rather than abandoning them,

WE CAN TAKE STEPS TO DEAL WITH REGULAR DISRUPTION OF OUR PLANS.

We will see how that can be done in looking at each of the examples.

6. Coping with the Unexpected

6.1. Accidents

Hopefully, this is a very rare occurrence in your firm.

Under your firm's health and safety policy both you and your workteam should know how to

REDUCE THE LIKELIHOOD OF ACCIDENTS TAKING PLACE.

Even if accidents are very rare, you and your team should know what to do if one happens. At the very least you should know the location of the nearest first-aid box and how to fetch help. If the accident is serious, as a supervisor, you should know the procedures within the firm for entering an accident report.

So, you must deal with the accident effectively and

REDUCE THE DISRUPTIVE EFFECT IT MAY HAVE ON YOUR TEAM AND YOURSELF.

Depending on the seriousness of the accident this may simply be one of those days when all or some of your

PLANS CANNOT BE ACHIEVED.

6.2. Machinery Breakdown

Whether you are supervising a workteam that uses machines for mass-production, computers, typewriters, check-out tills, dry-clean equipment, ovens or lawnmowers, it is likely that you are dependent upon some machinery, or tools. The breakdown of this machinery may be a fairly common occurrence — especially if it is old.

The key question is

IS THIS A REGULAR TIME WASTER?

If the answer to this question is 'yes', then it is worth thinking about what you can do to reduce the time lost on a long-term basis.

For example, to REDUCE the likelihood of this happening, could you:

press for more regular servicing of machines?

make a case for buying new machines?

To reduce the disruption caused by machinery breakdown could you:

arrange a system so that breakdown engineers arrive as quickly as possible?

make sure your workteam know exactly what to do when a breakdown occurs?

This may avoid time lost as the workteam stand around waiting for new instructions, or waiting for you before they contact breakdown engineers.

If machinery breakdown occurs very rarely, then it may not be worth investing the time it takes to carry out the measures I have suggested. A breakdown may occasionally wreck your plans for the day, but not much time is lost in the long term.

6.3. Absences

Problems may be caused by the absence of one of your team, or the absence of someone else on whom you are relying.

The same rules apply here as for the breakdown of machinery.

SELF CHECK 10   TIME GUIDE 2 MINUTES

What is the key question we asked concerning the breakdown of machinery?

_____

RESPONSE CHECKOUT

The key question is — *is this a regular time waster?*

If it is, then it is worth investing some time in trying to:

reduce the likelihood of it happening;

reduce the disruption when it does happen.

PART

ACTIVITY 29

TIME GUIDE 10 MINUTES _____

I made some suggestions about how to put this into practice when it involved the breakdown of machinery. Think about what you can do when it involves the absence of a member of your team. Write down a few ideas in the space below.

_____

_____

_____

_____

Here are some suggestions. Not all of them apply in your case. Together with your ideas they may help you to cope with this problem when it arises.

Sometimes the absence is foreseeable, as when a member of your workteam has a doctor's or a dentist's appointment, and this should be taken into account in your work planning.

Can your workteam do one another's job? This may reduce the disruption of a key worker being absent. Job rotation can increase the interest of workers, too, but whether you will be able to do this depends on union agreements, the attitudes of members of your team and the complexity of the job. If you are going to do this, it is a good idea to do it in advance, so that someone is not thrown in at the deep end when an absence occurs.

Can you get a replacement easily and quickly? A system for getting a temporary replacement is worth thinking about if absenteeism is a regular problem. Together with job rotation this may solve your problem.

Reorganise your workeam (and yourself) so that the jobs which don't get done are those which are low in urgency and low in importance.

If you are going to miss deadlines it is usually better to notify people of this in advance.

As with accidents, we may have to accept that our *PLANS FOR THE DAY CANNOT BE ACHIEVED.*

6.4. Something Which You Had Planned To Do Takes Much Longer Than Expected

We considered this at the end of Part B. Basically, we agreed that we had to make a decision in this case: to continue with what we were doing, or to leave it and go on to something else.

PART If this is a REGULAR TIME WASTER, though, we can do more than this.

ACTIVITY 30

TIME GUIDE 3 MINUTES

What can you do if your estimates are regularly wrong?

_____

_____

_____

_____

If your estimates are regularly wrong, you can try two ways of making them more accurate and less likely to disrupt your own and your workteam's work.

Leave some flexibility in your time plan to allow for mistakes in your estimates. This is an especially good idea when you have to do something which is out of the ordinary and also important. *Over*-estimate rather than *under*-estimate how long it is going to take.

Make your estimates more accurate by checking back with your list at the end of the day. Compare your estimates with how long each task actually took. Next time your estimates may be more realistic.

6.5. Someone Gives You Something Else To Do

Remember that we gave you an example of this at the end of Part B? An approach that was suggested there was to:

discuss the importance of the new task against the importance of the task you had planned.

If the answer to the KEY QUESTION is: 'Yes, this is a regular time-waster', then you should think about what you can do to REDUCE the likelihood of this happening and REDUCE the disruption caused when it does. Consider this example:

Before

Jean was a young woman in charge of a small team of clerical staff. Her boss was forever passing work to her marked 'urgent', and setting deadlines which meant a great deal of disruption to the team's activities. Jean was a conscientious person who tried to get through all the work she was given. She sometimes grumbled and sometimes protested about the arrival of another 'urgent' piece of work, but she did the best she could to deal with it.

PART

After

Jean started to keep a simple log of the items her team was doing. She kept these on pieces of file card on her desk. They were useful for planning and also for when an 'urgent' piece of work arrived. If something urgent arrived when Jean and the team were very busy, she would take the current cards to her boss, show him the workload and explain what effect doing the task would have on the rest of her work.

ACTIVITY 31

TIME GUIDE 10 MINUTES

What effects do you think this would have on Jean's boss and the number of pieces of 'urgent' work which arrived for her to do?

_____

_____

_____

_____

This is a real-life example and the effects it had were:

fewer pieces of urgent work arrived, as the boss came to appreciate how much work Jean's team were doing;

the boss tended to consult Jean more, and warn her when urgent and important projects were likely to arrive;

Jean got more control over her own time and the time of her workteam.

This was because Jean had the facts at her fingertips and could argue on the basis of evidence and effects.

You may have suggested that the boss began to look more closely at how Jean organised her workteam.

This might have happened, but Jean was confident that they were well organised. If the boss had shown an interest in this, Jean was prepared to state a case for more people and for better equipment.

Another suggestion may have been that relations between Jean and the boss got worse.

This might have happened if Jean had been aggressive or had refused to do urgent work, but she made her case very reasonably on the basis of the workload.

PART

You may have suggested that it had no effect on the number of pieces of urgent work arriving.

52

In fact this tactic ALWAYS has an effect EITHER on the amount of urgent work arriving, OR on the resources which are made available to do it, AND/OR the amount of notice we are given.

We have looked at five examples of unexpected events taking place which can ruin our best-laid plans. They were:

accidents;

machine breakdown;

absences;

under-estimating time needed;

extra work.

These were chosen as the five most common examples of unplanned problems.

SELF CHECK II   TIME GUIDE 5 MINUTES

a) In dealing with machine breakdown, absences, under-estimates, or extra work, what is the key question we need to ask ourselves?

_____

b) If the answer to the key question is 'yes', what do we need to do?

_____

_____

RESPONSE CHECKOUT

a) Is this a regular time-waster?

b) Find a long-term solution which will REDUCE the likelihood of it occurring. REDUCE the damage when it does.

PART

We have been looking at time planning, and how you might make your plans more effective.

If much of your job is routine then you will need to invest less time in planning, and the plans you make are much more likely to be achievable.

For non-routine jobs it is both:

more necessary to plan your time;

more difficult to do so accurately.

Do not be discouraged if at first you do not succeed. Begin with flexible plans and gradually aim to make them more accurate. Consider your objectives very carefully.

7. Dealing with Time Management Problems

The final sections contain some advice about dealing with time management problems. They may be helpful as they stand, or they may be helpful in giving you ideas about how to cope with your own particular problems.

EXTENSION 3
page 68

7.1. Time Logs

We saw, in Jean's case, how the use of evidence — facts and figures — can help in arguing for a decision which we see as sensible.

Our key question when our plans are disrupted was: is this a regular time waster? In order to answer this question we need to have a firm grasp of the facts.

One way of doing this is to use a time log.

Simple Time Logs

A simple time log would just be a piece of paper on which you note everything you have done in the course of the day, and the amount of time you spent doing it. Use a fresh piece of paper for each day.

It will need to be quite detailed and quite accurate.

Complex Time Logs

There are a number of different formats for complex time logs. Here is an example. It includes space for a daily plan, a space for activities, the purpose of those activities, time taken on them and whether or not they were anticipated. It also includes a space to be filled in about achievements and matters to be taken up (to deal with problems).

PART

Plan: Tick items achieved			Day: Date: Page number:
Time	Activity	Tick if anticipated	Purpose
Achieved:(apart from planned items)	Problems		Action

PART

55

ACTIVITY 32

TIME GUIDE 5 MINUTES

Think for a few moments about the ADVANTAGES of keeping a time log. Then think about the DIFFICULTIES. Write your ideas in the space below.

ADVANTAGES _____

_____

DISADVANTAGES _____

_____

The advantages may be that you have an accurate record of how you have used your time.

This can help you in:

better planning;

identifying areas of waste;

presenting a case to your manager about waste, the workload or other problems.

The difficulties may be:

it takes time to fill in the log;

it is an extra chore to do;

you will need to do it throughout the day. You will need to do it either continuously or at hourly intervals, otherwise you will forget what you have done and it will not be accurate.

If you think there are many advantages which apply to you, and that you can overcome the difficulties, it is worth trying to keep a time log. Keep a log for two weeks, or for a month, and then look at the entries and add up where all the time has gone.

There is a third type of time log.

Specific Time Logs

These are used for particular projects or problems, to keep track of waste or to help with planning. You may keep one, for example, to keep account of how much time is wasted through machinery breakdowns, or how much time is spent on a particular order.

Because they are not as comprehensive as other types of time log, specific logs are easier to keep. They may prove valuable in understanding how your time is spent and in explaining this to others.

PART
C

56

SELF CHECK 12

a) What are the three types of time log?

_____

_____

_____

b) What are the *two* main uses of time log information?

_____

_____

RESPONSE CHECKOUT

a) The three types of time log are *simple*, which is just a note of what you did and how long it took; *complex* which provides a more detailed breakdown of what you did, how long it took and whether you achieved your objectives; *specific*, which you might use to record time spent on a particular project.

b) The main uses you can make of the information are to understand how time was used and as evidence when you're explaining your use of time to other people.

8.   Getting Time Management Accepted

ENSION 4
e 68

We have seen that the scope of time management is very broad. It embraces:

making decisions about your goals and objectives;

analysing demands on your time;

analysing how your time is spent;

planning your time;

negotiating with others over how you spend your time.

In fact, there are many things which will affect the way you use your time, and the kind of demands which other people place upon it.

PART

57

Consider this final case.

Tom was a supervisor in charge of a team of maintenance engineers in a factory. He had been in this job for two months when he became interested in time management as a solution to his problems. He tried a series of time logs, and new systems to try to get control of his time and the time of his team. He enjoyed only limited success.

It turned out that the factory manager encouraged people to approach members of Tom's team directly, and get them to do maintenance jobs. The factory manager himself did this frequently. This meant that Tom often did not know what his team were doing, and his plans for preventative maintenance were often disrupted.

The factory manager would not listen to Tom's reasonable arguments about the importance of particular jobs, and did not support any new system Tom proposed.

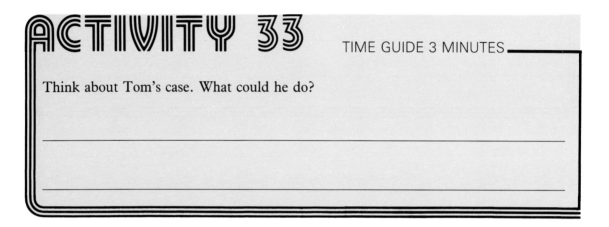

ACTIVITY 33   TIME GUIDE 3 MINUTES

Think about Tom's case. What could he do?

_____

_____

There are a number of alternatives in Tom's case, some of them quite drastic. He could:

look for another job;

have a showdown with the factory manager.

Tom thought these were *too* drastic.

EXTENSION 5
page 69

The causes of the problem here were:

STRUCTURAL — who had the power to give instructions to Tom's team? Tom thought all requests should go through him. But the previous maintenance supervisor had obviously allowed *anyone* to give his team instructions;

PERSONALITIES — the factory manager would not listen to Tom's reasoned argument.

What could Tom do? He could:

work on building a good relationship with his team, so that they would keep him informed of what was happening;

PART

talk to his team about priorities, and get agreement about the importance and urgency of matters;

talk to the people who make demands on his team to ensure that the demands go through him so that he can try to foresee some of the demands;

work on persuading the factory manager to consult him more;

deal with the main result of his time management problems (which is STRESS).

These are all practical options. Check to see if your suggestions were similar to these — can you see why it is reasonable to try to put all of these into effect?

Tom's problems were REGULAR disruptions. It was necessary, therefore, to invest some time to REDUCE the likelihood of them occurring and REDUCE the disruption when they did occur.

And Tom had to accept that:

getting control of his time was going to be a slow and gradual process;

most of the work was going to involve talking with and persuading other people.

So time management problems can often involve

NEGOTIATION

or

CONFLICT.

Even when we have sorted out our own priorities.

Time management problems are often affected by RESOURCES, too. Many time management problems could be solved by:

an extra machine;

an extra pair of hands;

more money spent on the job.

Generally, the steps to take are:

in the SHORT TERM, manage with what you have, accepting that some things will not get done;

prepare a case, for the LONG TERM, for extra resources, on the basis of evidence and facts.

Solving time management problems can have an effect upon resources. If it is possible in your situation it is worth thinking about what you can DELEGATE to members of your team. Training people to do the jobs you delegate to them can take time, but it is often worth doing in the long term.

SELF CHECK 13

a) Which of the following can sometimes be necessary to deal with time management problems? Tick the ones you think are applicable.

Deciding objectives	Negotiating
Discussing priorities	Team building
Analysing demands	Delegation
Analysing how time is spent	Planning
Making a case for more resources	Handling conflict

b) When should we look for SHORT-TERM and LONG-TERM solutions to time management problems?

_____

_____

RESPONSE CHECKOUT

a) All of these activities may be needed at some stage in dealing with different problems.

b) We need to look for SHORT-TERM solutions if a problem occurs regularly or if we can foresee one occurring in the future. We need to look for LONG-TERM solutions if people are going to need a lot of persuasion about the effectiveness of time management, or if your plan involves changing the use of resources.

9. Summary

● PLANNING

    —a DIARY   helps with long-term planning:

                          appointments;

                          future commitments.

    —a LIST   helps with short-term planning;

                          deciding the order of work;

                          deciding how much time to spend;

keeping track of several jobs at once;

planning the next step in a long series;

jogging your memory.

● ORDER PLANNING　　　　—make decisions on the basis of:

urgency;

importance.

● PLANS CANNOT ALWAYS BE ACHIEVED

—but even partially achieved plans may be useful and any plan helps to make better decisions when the unexpected occurs.

● DEAL WITH REGULAR DISRUPTION OF PLANS:

—identify regular time-wasters by using a log;

find a long-term solution which reduces the likelihood of their happening;

reduce the possibility of damage when they do occur.

● TIME LOGS　　　　—provide evidence on how you are actually using time;

the information they contain may help you to get the idea of time management accepted in your workplace.

PART

PART D
PERFORMANCE CHECKS

1. End Check

Time guide
60 mins You may now review your understanding of the unit as a whole by completing this group of questions. DON'T GUESS THE ANSWERS — if you're not sure, flick back into the unit and check before writing anything.

TRUE/FALSE

Respond to each statement by writing TRUE or FALSE in the space provided.

1. Managing time involves spending more time on the important parts of your job. _____

2. Crises occur even in the best of firms. _____

3. Our time often gets used up in responding to demands which other people place on us. _____

4. We should never do things just out of habit. _____

5. Something is urgent when it is top priority. _____

6. Jobs in the planning square may not get done because they are not urgent. _____

7. Once you have started a job you should always finish it, regardless of how long it takes. _____

8. Plans can help us make better decisions when faced with the unexpected. _____

PART

COMPLETION

Complete each sentence with a suitable word or words.

9. In order to manage our time we need to think about what we are trying to _____ and what stands in the way of our _____.

10. Crisis management brings with it the twin problems of _____ and _____.

11. Becoming better at managing our time means making _____ _____ more and more of it.

12. The FIVE stages in making a decision are:

   1) _____.

   2) Objectives Stage.

   3) _____.

   4) _____.

   5) Action Stage.

13. Good habits can help to make the _____ _____ of our time.

14. Something is important when it will have a _____ _____ upon our job.

15. The main thing we gain from the time management grid is that we do not confuse _____ with _____.

MULTIPLE CHOICE

Respond to each question by putting a mark against the answer that is most correct.

16. Which ONE of the following statements best describes time management?

   a) Managing our time means avoiding crises and doing our job carefully.

   b) Managing our time means getting more done in the same amount of time.

   c) Managing our time means getting more control over how we spend our time and then making sensible choices about how we use it.

   d) Managing our time means doing urgent things in advance of deadlines and giving more time to the important part of our job.

PART

17. Which ONE of the following statements best describes the activity trap?

    a) There always seems to be too many things to do, and not enough time to do them all.

    b) We spend most of our time responding to demands upon us without thinking about what we are trying to achieve.

    c) We spend most of our time on unimportant aspects of our job.

    d) We are unable to get agreement on what our objectives and priorities should be.

18. Which ONE of the following statements best describes something which is urgent?

    a) It has to be done by a specific time, shortly in the future, although it may not be very important.

    b) It is something small and easy to do and should be done right away before we forget it.

    c) It is something important which unexpectedly arises.

    d) It is something in the planning square of the time management grid.

19. Which ONE of the following questions should we ask to see if we should take LONG-TERM action over something which has disrupted our plans?

    a) Is it important?

    b) Is this a regular time-waster?

    c) Do I need more resources?

    d) Who could I give this job to?

20. Which ONE of the following statements best describes the importance of thinking about alternatives in making a decision?

    a) Because there is always more than one way of doing a thing.

    b) Because it reminds us that we control how we spend our time, by making decisions.

    c) Because we may save time in this way.

    d) Because it is a stage in making a decision which we must always go through.

AUDIO TAPE
Side 2
Time guide
35 mins
PART
D

END CHECK — CHECKOUT

The answers and explanations for these End Checks are on Side 2 of our Audio Tape. Have your responses with you as you play this tape. As you listen you can check how well you have done and make notes as you proceed.

2. Tutor Check

Read the following case and then deal with the accompanying questions.

John is a supervisor in a busy engineering firm. He is in charge of a team in the machining department. The department works on a batch-production basis. Orders are passed down to the supervisors, the equipment is re-set and the batch is produced.

Part 1

Recently there have been problems in reaching deadlines, and overtime has been authorised. Three times in the past week John has gone home late and tired, and fallen asleep in the armchair in front of the television. On one occasion he missed his son's sports day at school because of unexpected overtime.

The machining department manager was concerned about the regular failure to meet deadlines. He called the supervisors together and told them that they would have to get the men to work harder on the orders and police coffee breaks more strictly. John wasn't convinced that this would solve the problem. Nor were the other supervisors, though none of them said so.

Part 2

John went back to his section, thinking over what had been said in the meeting. He had a word with each member of his team in the course of the day, and told them that the manager might be keeping an eye on them.

Their reactions varied. Some of them said that they would not be willing to work overtime in future if that was the firm's attitude. John would have liked to spend more time discussing the matter with them, but it was a day when he was much in demand. Quality control and stores both wanted to have their monthly discussions, and John had to leave the team to get on with their job.

You only need to write ONE or TWO sentences against each question.

1. In Part 1 of the case:

   a) What TWO objectives might John be failing to achieve?

   b) What might be the causes of the failure to meet deadlines? List THREE things, not including the possibility that the men are not working hard enough.

   c) What kind of evidence could John, or one of the other supervisors, use to show that there was another cause to failing to meet deadlines.

2. In Part 2 of the case:

   a) What decision does John have to take about how to spend his time in the afternoon? List THREE opinions he might have. Which would you choose?

   b) How could John go about collecting evidence to find the cause of the time management problems?

PART

65

3. Work-based Project

Time guide
60 mins

This section deals with how you can take steps to become a better manager of your time in your own workplace.

1. Go back to your response to Activity 13. Now that you know more about time management you may want to add to your answer.

2. Identify *two* problems which arise from the demands upon your time. You should choose problems which EITHER arise regularly, or which you expect to arise in the near future.

3. Make a list of the alternatives which are open to you in dealing with problems. List at least *three* alternatives for each problem.

4. Say what you intend to do about the problems, and why.

5. When either of your problems arises again, describe briefly whether your method of dealing with it was effective. If not, what else could you do?

PART E   UNIT REVIEW

1.   Return to Objectives

Now that you have completed your work on this unit, let us review each of our four unit objectives.

You will be better able to:

● **UNDERSTAND THE BENEFITS OF BETTER MANAGEMENT OF YOUR TIME.**

We saw some of the negative consequences of poor time management: stress, mistakes being made, frustration and a failure to take advantage of opportunities. Managing our time means doing something with it — achieving more of what we want to achieve. You know now that time management means thinking about our objectives, which takes us on to the second aim of the unit.

You will be better able to:

● **CLEARLY EXPLAIN THE PRIORITY OF DIFFERENT DEMANDS ON YOUR TIME.**

You should now be able to do this, in terms of relative urgency and importance. You should also be able to explain the particular danger which is likely to affect that demand, depending on which of the squares in the management grid it occupies.

The third objective was, you will be better able to:

● **SET OUT THE STEPS YOU CAN TAKE TO PLAN AND CONTROL YOUR TIME.**

You can list the demands likely to be made of you. You can begin to plan your time more accurately. You should be able to explain the advantages of planning, despite the fact that sometimes plans can't be achieved.

The fourth objective was, you will be better able to:

PART

● **ANALYSE PROBLEMS WHICH MAY ARISE AND EXPLAIN HOW YOU MIGHT DEAL WITH THEM.**

By now you will be aware of the importance of identifying and analysing recurrent, or regular, problems. These will need an investment of time to bring about long-term solutions.

I hope that this work you have done was enjoyable, that it has given you some good ideas about how to become a better manager of your time, and that you will continue in your studies.

2.   Extensions

There are more than a dozen books written on time management, but most of them are written for executives in businesses. The books I have listed below have been carefully chosen to make the best use of your reading time.

EXTENSION 1   Checklist: Checklist 1 — Effective Use of Executive Time

                        Publisher: British Institute of Management

EXTENSION 2   Book: *Just in Time*

                        Author: Rutherford, R D

                        Publisher: John Wiley and Sons

Although this is American, and is not written especially for supervisors, it is well laid out with hundreds of tips and ideas about how to manage your time.

EXTENSION 3   Book: *Time, The Essence* Vols I and II

                        Author: Austin, B

                        Publisher: British Institute of Management Foundation

There are two booklets which concentrate on the use of diaries and have time logs. Volume I explains the use of diaries and logs for better planning, Volume II contains blank forms which you could copy for use.

EXTENSION 4   Book: *Getting Things Done*

                        Author: Bliss, E C

                        Publisher: Elm Tree Books

An ABC approach to time management problems which is full of ideas.

Once you have identified a particular time management problem, of course, the solution may lie in better delegating, or better negotiating with your boss, or better communication. Your study tutor will be able to advise you on what to read.

Book: *Super Series Unit 107: Supervising with Authority*

Author: NEBSM/NRMC

Publisher: Pergamon Open Learning

If you're not sure whether you would have the authority to introduce time management plans which affect other people, you might find it useful to work through this unit.

These extension opportunities can all be taken up via your Support Centre. They will either have the materials or will arrange that you have access to the materials. However, it may be more convenient to check out the materials with your personnel or training people at work — they may well give you access. There are other good reasons for approaching your own people; for example, they will become aware of your interest and you can involve them in your development.

3.   References

Book: *Managing Time Effectively*

Author: Dingwall, R

Publisher: The Granary Press

Series: Management Action Programme Resource Library, part 5, number 4.

This is a booklet with questionnaires, problem diagnosis, and sections on better delegation and better communication.

This reference can be taken up via your Support Centre. They will either have the materials or will arrange that you have access to the materials. However, it may be more convenient to check out the materials with your personnel or training people at work — they may well give you access. There are other good reasons for approaching your own people; for example, they will become aware of your interest and you can involve them in your development.

If you do wish to make use of this reference then don't think that you must read it right through. Just dip into it for a slightly wider treatment of the topic raised by the unit.

PART

NEBSM RECOGNITION

IT IS IMPORTANT TO HAVE YOUR ACHIEVEMENT RECOGNISED

The National Examining Board for Supervisory Management (NEBSM) makes nationally recognised awards to supervisory managers who successfully complete its courses. If you study an appropriate selection of approved units in the Super Series and complete the NEBSM assessments successfully you can obtain NEBSM MODULE AWARDS which lead on to the CERTIFICATE IN SUPERVISORY MANAGEMENT. Some 6,500 of these are already awarded annually to students who have been successful on their courses. They come from a wide variety of industries — production, retail, catering, DHSS, Local Government and Police, to name but a few.

WHY NOT REGISTER WITH NEBSM NOW?

All you have to do is complete the registration form in this unit and send it with your registration fee to NEBSM and we will record your details on computer. We will send you your PASSPORT to a NEBSM AWARD and details of the procedure to be followed in order to obtain NEBSM MODULE AWARDS and the full NEBSM CERTIFICATE. We cannot answer queries arising from the Unit, but we can give information about further Units, Support Centres and NEBSM AWARDS.

Please contact: NEBSM OPEN LEARNING,
76 Portland Place,
LONDON,
W1N 4AA

ORGANISATIONS

Organisations concerned with training in any type of industry may use this material to construct their own training courses.

Membership and Professional Bodies may wish to recognise units, or groups of units for fulfilment, or part fulfilment of the educational requirements of their qualifications.

SUPPORT CENTRES

ASHINGTON, NORTHUMBERLAND TECHNICAL COLLEGE (0670) 813248
BALLYMENA TECHNICAL COLLEGE (0266) 2871/4
BATHGATE, WEST LOTHIAN COLLEGE OF FURTHER EDUCATION (0506) 634300
BEDFORD COLLEGE OF HIGHER EDUCATION (0234) 51671
BELFAST, COLLEGE OF TECHNOLOGY (0232) 227244
BIRMINGHAM, HALL GREEN TECHNICAL COLLEGE (021) 778 2311
BOSTON COLLEGE OF FURTHER EDUCATION (0205) 65701
BRADFORD AND ILKLEY COMMUNITY COLLEGE (0274) 753000
BRIDGEND COLLEGE OF TECHNOLOGY (0656) 55588
BRIDGWATER COLLEGE (0278) 55464
BURTON UPON TRENT TECHNICAL COLLEGE (0283) 45401
CANTERBURY COLLEGE OF TECHNOLOGY (0227) 66081
CARDIGAN COLLEGE OF FURTHER EDUCATION (0239) 612032
CARLISLE TECHNICAL COLLEGE (0228) 24464
CASTLEFORD, WAKEFIELD DISTRICT COLLEGE (0977) 554571
CHESTER COLLEGE OF FURTHER EDUCATION (0244) 677677
CLYDEBANK COLLEGE (041) 952 7771
COLCHESTER INSTITUTE (0206) 570271
COSHAM, HIGHBURY COLLEGE OF TECHNOLOGY (0705) 38131
COVENTRY TECHNICAL COLLEGE (0203) 57221
CRAWLEY COLLEGE OF TECHNOLOGY (0293) 512574
CREWE AND ALSAGER COLLEGE OF HIGHER EDUCATION (0270) 583661
CROYDON COLLEGE (01) 688 9271/6
DARLINGTON COLLEGE OF TECHNOLOGY (0325) 467651
DERBYSHIRE COLLEGE OF HIGHER EDUCATION (0332) 47181
DUNDEE COLLEGE OF COMMERCE (0382) 29151
DURHAM, NEW COLLEGE (0385) 62421
EDINBURGH, STEVENSON COLLEGE OF FURTHER EDUCATION (031) 453 6161
ENNISKILLEN, FERMANAGH COLLEGE OF FURTHER EDUCATION (0365) 22431
EPSOM, NORTH EAST SURREY COLLEGE OF TECHNOLOGY (01) 3941731
GATESHEAD TECHNICAL COLLEGE (0632) 4771714
GLASGOW, STOW COLLEGE (041) 332 1786/7/8/9
GLENROTHES AND BUCKHAVEN TECHNICAL COLLEGE (0592) 772233
GRAYS THURROCK, THURROCK TECHNICAL COLLEGE (0375) 71621
GREAT YARMOUTH COLLEGE OF FURTHER EDUCATION (0493) 655261
GUILDFORD COLLEGE OF TECHNOLOGY (0483) 31251
HALIFAX, THE PERCIVAL WHITLEY COLLEGE OF FURTHER EDUCATION (0422) 58221
HAWICK, THE BORDERS COLLEGE OF FURTHER EDUCATION (0450) 74191
HEREFORDSHIRE TECHNICAL COLLEGE (0432) 267311/6
HUDDERSFIELD POLYTECHNIC (0484) 22288
HULL, HUMBERSIDE COLLEGE OF HIGHER EDUCATION (0482) 41451
INVERNESS COLLEGE OF HIGHER AND FURTHER EDUCATION (0463) 236681
LEICESTER, WIGSTON COLLEGE OF FURTHER EDUCATION (0533) 885051
LONDON CORDWAINERS TECHNICAL COLLEGE (01) 9850273/4
LONDON HACKNEY COLLEGE (01) 9858484
LONDON (SOUTH WEST) COLLEGE (01) 677 8141
MACCLESFIELD COLLEGE OF FURTHER EDUCATION (0625) 27744
MANCHESTER (CENTRAL) COLLEGE (061) 831 7791
MANCHESTER (GREATER), TAMESIDE COLLEGE OF TECHNOLOGY (061) 339 8683
MANSFIELD, WEST NOTTINGHAMSHIRE COLLEGE OF FURTHER EDUCATION (0623) 27191
NEWCASTLE COLLEGE OF ARTS AND TECHNOLOGY (091) 273 8866

NEWPORT, ISLE OF WIGHT COLLEGE OF ARTS AND TECHNOLOGY (0983) 526631
NORTHAMPTON, BLACKWOOD HODGE MANAGEMENT CENTRE/NENE COLLEGE (0604) 719531
NORWICH CITY COLLEGE OF FURTHER AND HIGHER EDUCATION (0603) 660011
OXFORD COLLEGE OF FURTHER EDUCATION (0865) 512574
PLYMOUTH COLLEGE OF FURTHER EDUCATION (0752) 264746
PONTYPRIDD, POLYTECHNIC OF WALES (0443) 405133
PRESTON, LANCASHIRE POLYTECHNIC (0772) 22141 .
REDDITCH COLLEGE (0527) 63607/8/9
ROCHDALE, STATE MILL CENTRE (0706) 527102
SHEFFIELD, STANNINGTON COLLEGE (0742) 341691
SLOUGH COLLEGE OF HIGHER EDUCATION (0753) 34585
SOLIHULL COLLEGE OF TECHNOLOGY (021) 705 6376
SOUTHAMPTON INSTITUTE OF HIGHER EDUCATION (0703) 29381 and 28182
SOUTH SHIELDS, SOUTH TYNESIDE COLLEGE (0632) 560403
ST. HELENS COLLEGE OF TECHNOLOGY (0744) 33766
STOCKTON–BILLINGHAM TECHNICAL COLLEGE (0642) 552101
STOKE-ON-TRENT, CAULDON COLLEGE OF FURTHER EDUCATION (0782) 29561
SUNDERLAND, MONKWEARMOUTH COLLEGE OF FURTHER EDUCATION (0783) 487119
SWINDON COLLEGE (0793) 40131
THURSO TECHNICAL COLLEGE (0847) 66161
WATFORD COLLEGE (0923) 41211/6
WEST ANGLIA TRAINING ASSOCIATION LIMITED (0480) 76690
WEST BROMWICH, SANDWELL COLLEGE OF FURTHER AND HIGHER EDUCATION (021) 5569010
WIGAN COLLEGE OF TECHNOLOGY (0942) 494911
WORCESTER, EVESHAM COLLEGE OF FURTHER EDUCATION (0905) 41151
WORCESTER TECHNICAL COLLEGE (0905) 28383
YORK COLLEGE OF ARTS AND TECHNOLOGY (0904) 704141

This list is correct at the time of publication of the unit. If you do not find a Centre near you, please contact NEBSM for the latest list.

THE SUPER SERIES

PRINCIPLES AND PRACTICE OF SUPERVISION

100 Needs and Rewards
101 Enriching Work
102 Workteams
103 Team Leading
104 Leading Change
105 Organisation Systems
106 Supervising in the System
107 Supervising with Authority
109 Taking Decisions

TECHNICAL ASPECTS OF SUPERVISION

200 Looking at Figures
202 Using Graphs
203 Method Study
204 Easy Statistics
205 Quality Control
207 Controlling Output
208 Value Analysis
209 Quality Circles
210 Computers
211 Stores Control
212 Managing Time
213 Descriptive Statistics
215 Supervisors and Marketing

COMMUNICATION

300 Communicating
301 Speaking Skills
302 Writing Skills
303 Communication Systems
304 Orders and Instructions
305 Project Preparation

ECONOMIC AND FINANCIAL ASPECTS

400 Accounting for Money
401 Control via Budgets
402 Cost Reduction
403 Wage Payment Systems
404 The National Economy
405 Cost Centres

INDUSTRIAL RELATIONS

500 Training Plans
501 Training Sessions
502 Discipline and the Law
504 Health and Safety
505 Industrial Relations in Action
506 Equality at Work
507 Hiring People
508 Supervising and the Law

FORM No. OL/50

OPEN LEARNING

76 PORTLAND PLACE
LONDON, W1N 4AA
TELEPHONE: 01-580 3050

REGISTRATION FORM FOR OPEN LEARNING STUDENTS

PLEASE USE CAPITAL LETTERS

SUPPORT CENTRE _____

SURNAME	FORENAMES (Initials are not acceptable)	SEX	AGE	Number of Years in Supervisory capacity — if any	Name of Employer if appropriate	Type of Industry

Address _____

_____

_____

Signed: _____

Date: _____

I enclose a cheque for £5.00 made payable to NEBSS as Registration fee for a period of 3 years.

Please send me my Passport to a NEBSS Award.

For NEBSS use only	Registration No.

NEBSS
OPEN LEARNING

This Voucher entitles you to an initial FREE CONSULTATION at any of the Support Centres listed in this Unit.

Make contact with the Open Learning Tutor at the Centre and arrange a convenient time for an appointment

ONE FREE CONSULTATION